HISTORIC

COMMUNITIES

A Child's Day

Bobbie Kalman & Tammy Everts
Illustrations by Antoinette DeBiasi

 Crabtree Publishing Company

HISTORIC COMMUNITIES

Created by Bobbie Kalman

*For my mother, Betty,
for her love and confidence*

Editor-in-Chief
Bobbie Kalman

Writing team
Bobbie Kalman
Tammy Everts

Editors
David Schimpky
Lynda Hale
Petrina Gentile
Tammy Everts

Computer design
Lynda Hale

Illustrations
Antoinette "Cookie" DeBiasi: cover design,
pages 9, 10, 13, 14, 15, 19, 20, 22, 23, 24, 25,
26, 27, 29, 30, 31
Barb Bedell: cover
Tammy Everts: pages 12, 18, 21

Special thanks to
Scott Adamson, Melinda Merante, Shirley
Crinkovich, Marg Sharp, and the staff of
Genesee Country Museum, Leigh Adamson
and Brian Adamson (the models who appear
on the cover and throughout the book), and
Chandler Press (for the story *The Boy and
His Dog*, page 14-15)

Photograph credits
Jim Bryant: page 7 (both)
Marc Crabtree: cover, title page, pages 4,
5 (both), 8, 9, 11, 12 (both), 16, 17 (both),
28 (both), 30, 31
Ken Faris: page 6 (left)
Bobbie Kalman: pages 6 (right), 29

Color separations
Book Art Inc.

Printer
Worzalla Publishing

Published by
Crabtree Publishing Company

350 Fifth Avenue	360 York Road, RR 4	73 Lime Walk
Suite 3308	Niagara-on-the-Lake	Headington
New York	Ontario, Canada	Oxford OX3 7AD
N.Y. 10118	L0S 1J0	United Kingdom

Cataloging in Publication Data
Kalman, Bobbie, 1947-
  A child's day

(The historic communities series)
Includes index.
ISBN 0-86505-494-0 (library bound) ISBN 0-86505-514-9 (pbk.)
The day-to-day life of children in nineteenth-century North
American communities is explored through stories and activities.

1. Children - North America - 19th century - Juvenile literature.
2. Pioneer children - North America - Juvenile literature.
3. Frontier and pioneer life - North America - Juvenile literature.
I. Everts, Tammy, 1970- . II. Title. III. Series: Kalman, Bobbie,
1947- . Historic communities.

HQ781.K35 1994   j305.23'0971   LC 93-38037

Contents

A child's day

Goodness, John, wake up. It's five o'clock already!" Mother called upstairs. John opened his eyes. Through the small window in his bedroom he could see that the sky was still dark. John stretched quickly and jumped out of bed—the morning chores had to be done.

When his feet hit the warm floor, he was thankful it wasn't winter. In winter he had to hop from foot to foot to keep his toes from freezing. The water in his washbowl would be so cold that a thin layer of ice floated on the top! After dressing in his cotton shirt and comfortable trousers, John hurried downstairs and rushed out to the barn to join his father.

John's home does not have a sink or plumbing. Instead, John keeps a pitcher of water and a washbowl in his bedroom for washing his face and hands in the morning.

Morning chores

Together, Father and John milked the cows, cleaned the calf pens, and fed the livestock. After giving his pet calf a quick pat, John returned to the house for breakfast.

4

A hearty breakfast

In the kitchen, Mother and sister Emily bustled around the fireplace preparing breakfast. Soon Father came in, and the family sat down to a hearty breakfast of sizzling bacon, fried potatoes, hot buckwheat pancakes with sweet maple syrup, fresh bread and preserves, and donuts.

Time for school

John and Emily took the lunch box that their mother had prepared for them and walked the half-hour trek to school. There was a spelling bee that day, and Emily's team won, as usual. No one could spell as well as Emily. John was happy when the day was over because he hated to see Emily gloat!

Chores and dinner

After school, John enjoyed helping Father care for the animals. He spread fresh hay in the stalls of the cows, oxen, calves, pigs, and sheep so the animals could have soft, clean beds. He fed the animals and milked the cows. Finally, it was time for dinner.

Happy evenings by the fire

After dinner, Mother and Emily washed the dishes and cleaned the kitchen. Father sat by the fireplace and whittled a new handle for his axe. John played with some building blocks his father had made for him.

Evenings were a happy time when the family sat together around the fire and ate apples, beechnuts, and popcorn. At nine o'clock, everyone went to bed. They needed plenty of rest for the next busy day.

John takes a moment to pet his cow, Daisy. Daisy wonders if John has a tasty treat hidden in his hand.

John and Emily "horse around" on the family wagon. Giddyup!

A full, busy life

Early settler children had lives that were very different from those of boys and girls today. Difficult work was a part of every day. In order to have enough food and clothing, the entire family had to work hard. Boys and girls began to do chores as soon as they were able to walk and talk. Parents loved their children, but they were very strict. They had to be—a family needed cooperation and teamwork to get everything done.

Using their imagination
Even though boys and girls worked hard, they always found time for fun. Many children today have a huge variety of toys, games, and activities from which to choose. Settler children had to

(left) "Idle hands are the devil's playground" was a common saying among the early settlers. Children did adult work such as caring for the oxen.

(right) Not every minute was devoted to work. Children played with simple but fun toys.

amuse themselves with simple games and a few homemade toys. Most of these games were played outdoors, using objects found around the farm or in the community. An old barrel hoop provided hours of fun when it was rolled with a stick. With a bit of pretending, a fence could be a bucking horse to ride. A sturdy board laid over a tree stump became a simple seesaw. Rocks, leaves, and branches created imaginary houses and forts. A child's only limit was his or her imagination.

A flurry of activity

A settler child's life was both difficult and fun, but it was never dull. From morning till night, each hour was a flurry of activity. An industrious childhood prepared children for the years of work that lay ahead.

(left) If a boy did not want to be a farmer, he became an **apprentice.** *He left his parents' house to live with a craftsperson, who taught him a trade such as making barrels or fine silver objects. This young boy is a blacksmith apprentice. One of his jobs is pulling the bellows to keep the fire hot.*

(right) Most girls learned skills, such as cooking, that they would need later as wives and mothers.

*Thirsty cows and horses need water to drink. John uses a **yoke** to carry water from the well to the barn. The yoke is worn across his neck and shoulders. It helps John carry loads that would be too heavy otherwise.*

All those chores!

John enjoyed working outside with Father. He, too, wanted to be a farmer when he grew up. Together they plowed fields, planted crops, tamed new horses, and hunted wild birds. It was John's job to bring the cows in from the pasture each night. This was a very important duty because wild animals could kill the valuable cows.

John forgets his duty

One Saturday, John and Emily went out to pick wild strawberries. They could eat as many berries as they wished while they were picking, as long as Mother had enough left to make a berry pie. John and Emily had a contest to see who could pick the most. They were so carried away by their competition that they lost track of the time. It seemed as if they had just eaten lunch when they heard Mother calling the family for supper.

Before bedtime that night, Father asked John if the cows had eaten a lot of grass in the pasture. Suddenly, John remembered that he had forgotten to herd the cattle back to the barn! He raced from the house to the faraway fields, listening to the wolves howling in the distance. John worried that he would be too late!

Luckily, the cows were safe. John was not as lucky, however. He had neglected his job. He knew he deserved the punishment Father would give him, but he did not look forward to it! What do you think John's punishment was?

Emily helps her mother spin thread, weave cloth, make candles, and sew clothing. In those days girls learned how to sew when they were young. By the time she was four years old, Emily had already stitched her first quilt square!

John hopes that he can get to the cows before the wolves do!

9

Potato cakes

Potato cakes are easy and fun to make. The early settlers liked them because they tasted good and used up leftover potatoes.

Divide day-old cold mashed potatoes into the number of servings you wish to make. Shape the potatoes into patties. Make sure the cakes are not too thick, or they will not cook in the middle. Heat oil or bacon fat in a frying pan. Place the potato cakes in the hot fat, turning them over when the first side is brown and slightly crispy. When both sides are cooked, serve your tasty, crusty potato cakes.

Time for dinner

It was finally dinnertime! The kitchen was warm and smelled good. John's stomach growled hungrily as Father said a prayer of thanks and served dinner. Emily and John received their servings last because, in those days, adults were always served first.

Finally, Father placed a heaping plate of food in front of each child. The plates were piled high with smoked ham, potato cakes, baked beans, butternut squash, johnny cake, and pickled beets. John's face lit up when he saw that Mother had prepared his favorite dish— fried apples 'n' onions!

Emily was not as happy to see the apples 'n' onions, which she didn't like at all. She did not complain, however. She was supposed to eat everything on her plate without arguing. The children ate quickly as they listened to their parents talk. Emily and John were not allowed to speak unless they were spoken to, but that didn't matter. Their hard work had made them too hungry to talk!

Using the recipes on these pages, you, too, can sample a taste of Emily and John's dinner. Make sure that you ask an adult to help with knives and the stove.

Fried apples 'n' onions

Believe it or not, apples and onions have an unusual and delicious flavor when cooked together!

8-10 slices of bacon
6 yellow onions
6 tart apples
2 tablespoons brown sugar

Fry the bacon slices in a skillet. While the bacon is cooking, peel and slice the onions. Remove the cores from the apples. Slice the apples into thin rings. Leave the skins on! They help the apples keep their shape, and the bright red adds color to the meal. When the bacon is completely cooked, remove it from the skillet and set it aside on a plate.

Drain most of the bacon fat from the skillet. Add the onion slices and cook them over medium-high heat for about three minutes. Spread the apple slices over the onions. Sprinkle brown sugar on top, cover the skillet, and cook for a few more minutes until the apples are tender. Stir only if it looks as if the onions are going to burn. Add the apples 'n' onions to the bacon. This dish serves six people.

It is Emily's job to make butter. **Churning** *the thick cream into soft butter is a hard job that takes hours, but someone has to do it! The fresh, delicious result is worth the effort.*

(opposite page) At the end of a long day's work, the family enjoys sitting down to a hearty dinner. Everyone is very hungry!

11

(left) Emily and John are ready for another school day.

(right) John has traced his hand in his copybook. He uses ink and a feather **quill** for writing. Oh, no! An ink blob has fallen on his drawing!

Some children had **slates**, which were like small blackboards. Students wrote on their slates with **slate pencils**.

Going to school

As early settler communities grew, people started thinking about their children's education. Parents wanted their children to be able to read the Bible so they would become better Christians. Learning to **cipher**, or do arithmetic, was necessary for children who were going to be farmers, craftspeople, millers, or storekeepers.

The one-room schoolhouse

After the morning chores were done, Emily and John started their long walk to school. The families in the area had built the new one-room building just a few months ago. The community was proud of its school, with its bright red paint and shiny new wood stove.

"Making their manners"

When Emily and John arrived at the school, Mr. Pennyworth, the teacher, was standing at the door. He smiled as they "made their manners," which meant bowing or curtsying to the teacher. Because nine-year-old John was one of the youngest boys in the class, he sat at the front of the boys' row of desks. Emily, who was fourteen, sat in the middle of her row.

An inky tale

One winter morning, as John was reading his **primer**, he heard the older boys behind him whisper and laugh. He tried to ignore them as he struggled to memorize the poems and Bible verses in his book. John wanted to practice writing the letters of the alphabet in his **copybook**, but he had to wait. The ink, which he had left in his desk overnight, had frozen after the stove fire was put out. Almost all the students had the same problem, so there was a row of thawing ink bottles along the top of the stove.

BANG! BANG! BANG! Huge booms filled the classroom. Many of the children screamed in terror, except the boys behind John, who laughed loudly. John saw that the ceiling was splattered with large black spots. Mr. Pennyworth noticed, too. As he glanced at the laughing boys, his face grew very serious. One by one, the mischief-makers were called outside by the teacher. When they came in, they were no longer laughing. Mr. Pennyworth had whipped them for leaving the corks in their thawing ink bottles on purpose to make them explode. The pranksters did not play tricks for quite a while after that!

13

Stories with a message

Emily and John loved to read. The books they read at home and school were very different from storybooks children read today. Their books were loaded with messages, or **morals**, about how people should behave. Morality tales were supposed to teach children kindness, good manners, and respect for others. There were no police in settler times, so people had to trust one

THE BOY AND HIS DOG

A FAVORITE DOG, named Mungo, stood by his mistress one morning as she prepared her children, Eliza and Edmund, for school.

Eliza had been busy assisting Edmund, who now stood waiting while his mother prepared his sister as quickly as possible. As it was getting late, she asked Edmund to fetch the lunch basket. This bad-mannered boy, however, only gave a sour look. Though he did not refuse, he did not hurry to obey his mother's order.

"Well, my son," she said, "If you are unwilling to do anything for others, how can you expect others to help you? Our Mungo would bring me the basket in a moment, if he knew how."

As the mother said this, which she meant only as a scolding for her son, she was surprised to see the dog go to the closet, take the basket down from behind the door, and bring it to her side.

another. Children were raised to be "good" and honest. In morality stories, good things happened to "good" children. Children who were considered "bad" always met with disaster.

The following story is taken from a third-grade school reader that might have been used by John and Emily. It tells the story of a boy whose dog had better manners than he did. How would you rewrite this story?

Let those children who are unwilling to help others, blush and be ashamed at the example of this noble dog.

Simple toys, simple joys

Most children did not have many toys, so they took very good care of the ones they had. Adults thought that some toys were meant just for boys and others for girls. Toy soldiers, metal pistols, and kites were considered playthings for boys. Dolls and dollhouses were toys just for girls. Both boys and girls loved to play with puppets, marbles, and jack-in-the-boxes.

Rolling a hoop with a stick is more difficult than it looks! John runs to keep up with his speeding hoop. Settler children used hoops from old wooden barrels for their games. Children had races to see who could keep their hoop rolling the longest.

New toys!

Emily and John were happy the day Father found time to make a pair of **stilts** for each of them. As John pictured himself walking tall on his stilts, Emily climbed on hers and was soon racing across the grass. She made walking on stilts seem easy. When John tried to mount his stilts, he was surprised to discover that it was more difficult than it looked! After falling off several times, he finally managed to take some slow, shaky steps.

Emily laughed, "You're so slow. I can walk circles around you." This made John angry and, before he knew what he was saying, he challenged his sister to a race.

The race begins

"On your mark… get set… GO!" Emily yelled, and off she raced. She was halfway across the field when she looked behind her to see how close John was. Emily gasped when she saw that John was lying on the ground with his stilts beside him! She jumped off her stilts and ran to help her brother. Emily worried that he might be badly injured.

John's clever trick

When she leaned over him to see if he was hurt, John leapt to his feet, jumped on his stilts, and started to zoom across the field. Emily was startled but began to giggle when she realized that John had tricked her. She laughed so hard that she could not finish the race. The children enjoyed the joke almost as much as they enjoyed their new stilts.

The birthday party

Mother pressed John and Emily's best clothes and told them to wash their faces. The children were going to Sarah Walker's birthday party! They had never been to a party before.

When they arrived at Sarah's house, several children were already there. Many of them had never been inside such a fancy house. Everyone sat nervously in Sarah's beautiful **parlor**. John and Emily were relieved when Sarah entered the room and greeted her guests. She suggested that they play **Blind Man's Buff**. Her guests agreed enthusiastically.

Blind Man's Buff

John was It, so he put on the blindfold. The other boys and girls joined hands and skipped in a circle around him. When John called "Stop!" everyone stopped and stood still. John pointed at a person in the circle—it was Emily! She entered the circle and tried to avoid John. Though he was blindfolded, John was very tricky. He quickly tagged Emily, but he still had to guess who she was. As John touched his sister's face and hair, he recognized the feel of the bow she was wearing in her hair. "Emily!" he shouted. Now Emily was It!

The children loved this game, and they played until everyone had a chance to be It. The afternoon flew by, and soon it was time for cake. The guests filed into Sarah's dining room and sat politely at the long table. No one said a word, but they were all very excited—beside each of their

Chocolate cake and juicy oranges make a tasty dessert. Oranges, which grow in tropical places, were expensive to ship to remote settler communities.

plates was an orange! The children weren't sure if they were allowed to eat it or if it was only meant as a decoration. When Mrs. Walker told them to enjoy their cake and orange, they couldn't believe their ears. The chocolate cake was delicious, but a sweet, juicy orange was a rare treat! Most children received this tropical fruit only at Christmas!

All too soon, it was time to go home. John and Emily remembered to thank Sarah and her mother for the lovely party. Then they raced home to tell Mother about the fun game, birthday cake, and delicious oranges.

Blind Man's Buff was the most popular parlor game in settler times. Children played it every chance they had.

Sunday—a special day

John and Emily's family went to church on Sunday morning. Sometimes the minister's sermon could be very long—up to three hours! After church, Emily and John were not allowed to work or play for the rest of the day. John could play with a toy model of Noah's Ark, but Emily was too old for such toys. For Emily, Sunday afternoons often seemed very, very dull.

Sunday was also called the **Sabbath.** *It was a day for resting and not doing work. Emily tries to sneak some work on her sampler when she knows she shouldn't. Don't get caught, Emily!*

Emily's secret work

Mother spent the day resting in the kitchen, Father sat outdoors, and John played on the floor. Emily wanted to finish the **sampler** she had been working on for months. She knew that she was not allowed to work on the Sabbath, but she couldn't understand why. She thought work was supposed to be good for her.

Hidden hands

Despite the rules, Emily decided she would do as she pleased this Sabbath. She sat in the parlor pretending to read the big family Bible, which was propped in her lap. Hidden behind the Bible, her hands were busy stitching the sampler!

An unfortunate mistake

Just before dinner, Emily's sampler was completed. It was beautiful, with tiny, neat, colorful stitches. She couldn't wait to show it to Mother. Emily didn't think Mother could be angry with her after seeing her lovely embroidery. She rose from her seat. Oh, no! By sewing so close to her lap to avoid being caught, Emily had sewn her sampler to her skirt!

The joke's on Emily!

John looked up at his sister and began to laugh. Mother and Father came into the room to see what was going on. When they saw Emily's predicament, they also started to chuckle. Emily had provided the entire family with a good laugh on a quiet day. This did not mean that she would not be punished, however. She would also have to start the sampler again. Emily learned quite a lesson!

Toy models of Noah's Ark were popular among young settler children. The Noah's Ark was the only toy with which they were allowed to play on Sunday. Parents thought that playing with this toy was a good Sabbath pastime because the tale of Noah and his ark was a Bible story.

Their Sunday best

Like most settler girls, Emily had only two outfits. During the week she wore a simple long dress, which she often covered with an apron to protect it from dirt and spills. Outdoors, Emily's bonnet protected her face and head from the hot sun. Emily was particularly careful about keeping her skin as light as possible. Women wanted their complexion to resemble **porcelain**, or fine china.

Sunday best

Emily loved to dress in fine clothing on Sundays and special holidays. Her best dress was made of **calico**. Calico was cotton cloth printed with a bright design. Petticoats puffed out her skirt. For two years Emily had worn this dress, and she was getting tired of it. She wanted to ask for a new velvet dress, but she knew that her parents did not have money for such a luxury.

When Emily's older cousin gave her a red velvet dress that no longer fit her, Emily could not believe her good fortune. Mother offered to help alter the dress to make it Emily's size, but Emily wanted to do it by herself.

A fashion mistake!

Finally, the dress was finished. Father, Mother, and John waited for Emily to come into the kitchen wearing her grand "new" dress. Emily entered the room, but she did not look happy. Somehow, she had made errors in taking measurements. The sleeves were different lengths, the waist was too tight, and the hem of the skirt was uneven. The dress was a disaster!

John hates dressing up in his good suit. His stockings, jacket, and trousers are all made of itchy wool. John prefers his comfortable everyday clothes!

Very young boys and girls were dressed alike in long cotton **smocks,** *or dresses, which were worn over loose trousers called* **pantalets.** *Around the age of four, a boy was* **breeched,** *which meant that he began to wear trousers like those of his father.*

Mother didn't make fun of Emily's mistakes. Instead, she complimented her on her tiny, neat stitching. She then offered once again to help Emily fix the dress. Together, mother and daughter sewed the hem, sleeves, and waist. When Emily tried her dress again, it fit perfectly. She was glad she had accepted Mother's help.

John liked how Emily looked in her dress, but he would find it hard not to giggle every time she wore it. The image of her first alterations would stay in his head for a long time!

Poor Emily! She tried to fix her dress, and everything went wrong. Emily is usually a good seamstress, but she was not quite ready for such a difficult challenge.

Mr. Cole pays a visit

A visit from someone who lived outside the community was always an exciting event. Settlers who had to travel often did so on horseback or by foot. When they were hungry or thirsty, they stopped at a friendly looking house and asked for a drink of water or a slice of bread. The travelers were asked to come in, given food, and invited to stay a while. The family was excited to hear news from other places.

Jingle, jingle, jingle

Down the road, a bell was ringing. Mother and Emily went to the door to see who was coming. John also heard the bell as he was working in the garden.

There was, indeed, a man driving a horse and wagon to the house. When he saw Mother, he waved his hand and called, "Hello!" It was the peddler, Mr. Cole, who had come to trade his wares for Mother's homemade candles, soap, and woven cloth. Mr. Cole traveled the countryside with his goods. He sold everything from pots and pans to toys and books. His wagon was a moving general store!

Goods, news, and jokes

The entire family was happy to see Mr. Cole. Mother knew that he would offer good prices on items the family needed. Father looked forward to hearing news from the other communities on Mr. Cole's route. Emily and John could not wait to hear Mr. Cole's funny jokes and stories. On his last visit, they had laughed until they cried!

A visit from the peddler was a big event. Itinerant shoemakers, tinsmiths, and scissors sharpeners, who traveled the countryside, were other welcome guests.

The tall-tale competition

At dinner that evening, Mr. Cole talked about a contest he had with a man in another town. The man had bet that he could tell more stories and jokes than Mr. Cole, and Mr. Cole had won the bet. John piped up, "My father knows a lot of stories. I bet he could have won that bet."

Mr. Cole's eyes twinkled. "Let's give it a try, son. If your father tells more tall tales than I do, I have some fine treats for you and your sister." The contest began. For every story or joke Mr. Cole told, Father also had a story or joke. John and Emily held their breath, hoping Father would win. Finally, Mr. Cole stopped.

A good sport

"I'm out of stories," he said. "You win!" From his bag of goods, Mr. Cole pulled a tin horn for John and a book for Emily. He also gave them each a small bag of candy! The children were proud of their father, but they felt badly for Mr. Cole, who had lost the contest.

"Cheer up," he told them, laughing. "Now I have one more story—I can tell folks about the time I was beaten at storytelling!"

Books, brushes, toys, and tools can all be found in Mr. Cole's wagon. John blows on his new horn as Emily reads her book. They will miss Mr. Cole when he leaves to continue on his route.

The country fair

After the autumn harvest, everyone looked forward to the country fair. John and his family were excited as they dressed in their Sunday best. Emily had entered some of her preserves in a contest and hoped to win a prize. John couldn't wait to see the horse races. Father looked forward to talking about crops and cattle with other farmers. Though she would be busy helping the women prepare the potluck fair dinner, Mother was happy to visit with her friends, whom she rarely saw.

An exciting race

The day passed quickly. The final event —the **thoroughbred** horse race—was approaching. Father explained to John that a thoroughbred was a purebred horse. The crowd at the racetrack admired the four beautiful horses with long legs and necks, glossy coats, and quick steps. John, Emily, and Father agreed that the thoroughbreds were certainly handsome!

Runaway horses!

BOOM! The gun went off, and the race began. John had never seen an animal run as fast as these horses! Suddenly, the horses veered off the track and raced through the crowd at full speed. Some mischievous boys had frightened them by throwing firecrackers at their feet. Now the horses were out of control and heading straight for the tent where the women were preparing dinner! The men in the crowd chased the horses, but the terrified animals were much too fast. Even their riders hung on for dear life!

John and Emily saw their mother come out of the tent, wondering what all the noise was about. They were very worried that Mother would be trampled by the racing horses. Mother had only seconds to react. As the horses approached, she flapped her apron at them. They were so startled that they changed direction and ran towards an open field, where their riders were able to bring them under control. As the horses calmed down, Mother looked up at the crowd, whose attention was now focused on her.

"What are you all looking at?" she asked. "Dinner's getting cold!"

Runaway horses are heading towards the tent where the fair dinner is to be held! Will anyone be able to stop them? What will happen to all the tasty food? Will Mother, who is standing right in the path of the horses, be run down?

The miller's cat has the important job of killing troublesome pests such as mice and rats.

As water runs over the mill wheel, the wheel turns and powers the huge millstones inside. The grain is ground between the stones as they spin in opposite directions.

A trip to town

Every autumn, Father took grain to the **gristmill** to be ground into flour. The gristmill was located outside the town. It used the power of fast-flowing water to operate its machinery. Mr. Harper, the gristmill owner, was a very important man in the community.

The fascinating gristmill

Sometimes Father let Emily and John come to the gristmill with him. Visiting the mill was exciting. Emily and John stared in awe at the complicated machinery. Emily liked to play with the mill cat. It was the cat's job to catch the mice and rats that ate the grain. Sometimes John and Emily stood on the miller's scale to see how much they weighed.

The blacksmith's forge

On some trips to town, Emily and John visited Mr. Reilly, the **blacksmith**. The blacksmith made everything from cooking utensils to nails and horseshoes. His workroom was an interesting place filled with many different tools and gadgets, such as hammers, mallets, tongs of all shapes and sizes, and an anvil.

John likes to watch the blacksmith work at the raised brick fireplace, called the **forge***. Mr. Reilly holds the iron in the fire with long tongs. When the iron is soft, he hammers it into horseshoes or tools on a heavy iron bench called an* **anvil***.*

When Mr. Reilly hits the red-hot metal, the sparks can fly!

To market, to market

Farmers made weekly trips into town to sell their goods, such as fruits and vegetables, meat and eggs, and baskets and quilts. Sometimes Father took Emily and John with him to help out at the market. It was an exciting place, filled with things to see and do. John wanted to watch a **cockfight**. Two roosters with spurs on their heels leapt at each other. Emily preferred the puppet show at the other side of the market square.

What luck!

Emily and John walked happily down the street. Father had told them they could visit the shops after they had unloaded the wagon. The children looked in shop windows, marveling at everything they saw.

As Emily was gazing through the newspaper office window, John spotted something shiny on the street. He bent and picked it up—a nickel! Before anyone could see him, he put it in his pocket. He didn't even show it to Emily. John imagined the big bag of candy he could buy for himself with a whole nickel. "Let's go to the general store," he said.

Inside the general store, the walls were lined with shelves that were filled with everything from cloth to tools. As Emily admired some fabric, John looked greedily at the candy jars. He could almost taste the **horehound** candy and licorice whips! He wanted some candy badly, but he began to feel guilty about spending the money he had found. John worried that using the nickel might be like stealing.

John spies a treasure on the street. What will he do with his shiny new nickel?

Emily admires the many beautiful fabrics available at the general store. She wishes she could have a colorful dress for each day of the week.

John's honesty pays off

John felt too guilty to spend the nickel, so he decided to tell Mr. Goodfellow, the shopkeeper, about the coin he had found. Mr. Goodfellow looked at John's anxious face and laughed. "As a matter of fact, young fellow, I lost a nickel as I was walking to the store this morning. You can keep it for being such an honest lad."

John was relieved. Mr. Goodfellow's words made him feel so good that he no longer wanted to be selfish. With the nickel, John bought a bag filled with his and Emily's favorite candies. On the ride home, John and Emily shared the candy as John told Father about his lucky nickel.

After John buys candy for himself and Emily, the two children enjoy a game of checkers at the general store. First John is winning, then Emily. In the end, the game is a tie!

A good life

John felt happy that night. He had an exciting day in town, a delicious supper waiting when he came home, and a special treat of candies that he had bought with his lucky nickel.

He felt cosy in his warm bed. Perhaps he and his father would go fishing tomorrow, after the chores were finished. He still had another week of summer vacation left and wanted to enjoy it as much as possible before school started again. Emily called "good night" to him from the next room. John smiled. Although he would never admit it, he was happy to have Emily as his sister.

John is content. He has a happy family and a good home. John works hard, but he also has lots of fun. Every day is a new adventure!

Glossary

bonnet A hat with strings that tie under the chin

buckwheat A type of grain

butternut squash A large, pear-shaped, yellowish-orange vegetable

complexion The color and texture of the skin on the face

curtsy A movement of respect made by girls or women; similar to a bow

embroidery Decorative sewing done with colored thread

horehound A plant used to flavor candy

industrious Hard working

itinerant Describing someone who travels from place to place

johnny cake A flat cake made of cornmeal and cooked on a flat pan

livestock Farm animals

needlework Sewing, knitting, or embroidery

noble Generous and dignified

parlor A sitting room, usually used for entertaining visitors

petticoat A dress-length undergarment worn beneath a dress or skirt

potluck A shared meal to which everyone brings food

predicament A difficult situation

preserves Fruits and vegetables treated with sugar or other additives to keep them fresh for a long time

sampler A piece of embroidery done in different stitches to show sewing skill

sin The act of breaking a religious law; doing something that is known to be wrong

skillet A flat frying pan

spurs Sharp prongs attached to the backs of roosters' feet during a cockfight

tongs A tool with two arms used for grasping objects

tropical Relating to the hot region near the equator

utensil An instrument or container used in the kitchen

wares Articles offered for sale

Index

2 3 4 5 6 7 8 9 0   Printed in U.S.A.   3 2 1 0 9 8 7 6 5 4

DATE DUE